Burning Profits:
10 Myths Destroying your Workforce.

Real strategies for Retention

and ROI

Elliot Evans

Copyright © 2023 Elliot Evans

All rights reserved.

ISBN: 9798877998391

Burning Profits

DEDICATION

Dedicated to all you 'chronic' warriors out there, fighting a war with their bodies every day for a shred of normality – you are amazing.

Also, to my Wife, the first person who saw me beyond my conditions
– I love you x

CONTENTS

Introduction 2
AGE 7
LAZINESS 13
DIVERSITY 18
BURDEN 23
CULTURE 27
ABSENTEEISM 33
MINDSET 39
HIGH COSTS 47
COMMUNICATION 54
RETENTION SAVES LIVES 58
About the chronic edge 63
About the Author 66
Bibliography 69

ACKNOWLEDGMENTS

A big thank you to Glenn Kirkham, whose advice sparked the idea for this book.

Thank you again to my Wife, for her constant reviewing of my work, ensuring my disability didn't impact on the readers' understanding and enjoyment of this book.

YOUR LIFE IS

OVER!

Introduction

Myth: "You will struggle to ever work in a regular job again."

Truth – "Watch me!"

It was back in 2017 when I first heard those words, I heard something similar back at school when I was around 12 years old, it was from an old schoolteacher, who said I'd struggle to achieve anything in my life as I didn't have either the intellect or drive to do so. This was at least 10 years before my Dyslexia diagnosis, and another 23 years before my Autism one. For me, those words fired up my drive to prove them wrong, but how many other children and young people had their dreams shattered by the words and actions of misunderstood preconceptions of achievement, without considering any underlying barriers?

Following my official diagnosis of Fibromyalgia (*a umbrella term much life dyslexia that has over 30 different symptoms ranging from inflammatory joint pain too bouts of Irritable Bowel Syndrome, often triggered by extreme mental or in my case physical trauma to the body, resulting in a change to the central nervous system that transmits messages throughout the body, although this is still a theory, with so much more to learn about the subject in general*), I was told I'd struggle to work again, ultimately ending a career in Social Work just before it began, ironically on the eve of my final placement, because at that time I believed them. I believed that the pain, the sickness, and the constant fatigue would last forever, but I was wrong, and by the time I realized, it was too late to go back without starting the course again from day one.

But why did they say that? Why did they believe that was I had got sick I would struggle to work again? Since that time I've worked full-time for two tech businesses in business development and for 3 different teams in the NHS, travelling to various locations across the whole of Lancashire and beyond, but still that myth about being able to work a regular job was so clear in that person of authorities mind, that it is understandable that so many others from HR departments to individuals going through the same as I did. The result? – Businesses lose experienced and quality employees and people lose their livelihoods leading them down a path of further inequality and poor health.

Throughout this book, I'm going to talk about 10 of the largest myths around ill-health and employment, the impact on both the individual and the business, and the truth behind the myth, to help others like me, stay or go onto having great careers, but helping businesses with their staff retention, awareness and knowledge which can lead onto better productivity and ultimately an increased profitability in the long-term.

Burning Profits

CHRONIC ILLNESS

IS FOR THE OLD.

Burning Profits

AGE

Myth: Chronic illness only affects older people.

Truth: Illness can affect people of all ages, including children and young adults.

Ill-health only impacts on old people, especially conditions such as arthritis and fibromyalgia so if staff do become sick, they may be close to retirement anyway, so it isn't too bad.

Unfortunately, that's not how life works and conditions such as these:

- **Fibromyalgia** - Fibromyalgia is a chronic disorder characterised by widespread musculoskeletal pain, fatigue, and tenderness in specific areas of the body. It is often accompanied by sleep problems, memory issues, and mood disturbances. The exact cause is unknown, but so believe it to involve a combination of genetic, environmental, and psychological factors, triggered by high stress or trauma. Currently, there is no medical cure for fibromyalgia, but treatment options such as medication, therapy, and lifestyle changes can help manage symptoms and improve quality of life for those affected by the condition.

- **Osteoarthritis** - Osteoarthritis is a common joint disease that causes the breakdown of the cartilage between the joints. This can lead to pain, swelling, and decreased mobility in the affected joints. It is often associated with aging, but it can also be caused by joint injury or overuse and can impact young people where it is named Youth Arthritis. Treatment typically involves managing symptoms through exercise, weight management, and medication. In severe cases, surgery may be necessary to repair or replace the damaged joint.

- **Rheumatoid Arthritis** – Rheumatoid arthritis is a chronic inflammatory disorder that affects the joints. It is an autoimmune condition, meaning the body's immune system mistakenly attacks its own tissues. This leads to pain, swelling, and stiffness in the affected joints, and over time can cause damage to the joint and surrounding tissues. The exact cause is not fully understood, some believe that it involves a combination of genetic and environmental factors. Treatment typically involves a combination of medication, physical therapy, and lifestyle changes to manage symptoms and prevent further joint damage.

- **Asthma** - Asthma is a chronic respiratory condition characterised by inflammation and narrowing of the airways, causing difficulty in breathing, wheezing, coughing, and chest tightness. It can be triggered by numerous factors such as allergens, pollution, and respiratory infections. Asthma cannot be cured, but it can be managed with medication and lifestyle changes to control symptoms and prevent asthma attacks.

- **ALS (Lou Gehrig's Disease)** - Lou Gehrig's Disease, also known as amyotrophic lateral sclerosis (**ALS**), is a progressive and fatal neurological disease. It affects nerve cells in the brain and spinal cord, leading to a loss of muscle control and eventually the ability to speak, eat, move, and breathe. The cause of the disease is still unknown, and there is currently no cure. Treatment mainly focuses on managing symptoms and improving the quality of life for patients.

- **Cancer** - Cancer is a disease characterised by the uncontrolled growth and spread of abnormal cells in the body. These cells can form tumours and interfere with the normal functions of organs and tissues. There are many different types of cancer, each with its own set of risk factors and treatment options. Some common risk factors for cancer include smoking, excessive alcohol consumption, and exposure to certain chemicals and radiation but the underlying cause is unknown. Treatment for cancer can include surgery, chemotherapy, radiation therapy, and targeted therapy, depending on the type and stage of the cancer. Early detection and treatment are crucial for improving the chances of survival and reducing the impact of cancer on the body.

- **COPD (Chronic Obstructive Pulmonary Disease)** - COPD, or chronic obstructive pulmonary disease, is a chronic lung condition that makes it difficult to breathe. It is often caused by long-term exposure to irritants such as cigarette smoke or air pollution. Symptoms include shortness of breath, wheezing, and chronic cough. COPD is a progressive disease with no cure, but treatment can help manage symptoms and improve quality of life.

- **Inflammatory Bowel Disease** - Inflammatory Bowel Disease (**IBD**) is a group of conditions that cause inflammation in the digestive tract. The two main types of IBD are Crohn's disease and ulcerative colitis, both of which can cause symptoms such as abdominal pain, diarrhoea, fatigue, and weight loss. IBD is a chronic condition that requires ongoing management and treatment to control symptoms and reduce inflammation in the intestines.

- **Cystic Fibrosis** - Cystic fibrosis is a genetic disorder that primarily affects the lungs and digestive system. It causes the production of thick, sticky mucus that can obstruct the airways and lead to respiratory difficulties. It also affects the pancreas, leading to difficulty in digesting food and absorbing nutrients. This condition is chronic and progressive, and there is currently no cure. Treatment focuses on managing symptoms and improving quality of life.

For example, mental health problems such as anxiety and depression are more prevalent among young adults than older adults. Similarly, some chronic conditions such as asthma and diabetes are more common in children and young adults than in older adults.

It is important to note that while ill-health can affect people of all ages, the type and severity of health problems can vary depending on age. For example, older adults are more likely to experience chronic conditions such as arthritis and heart disease.

It is important to take care of your health at all ages. This includes eating a healthy diet, getting regular exercise, and seeking medical attention when necessary. By taking care of your health, you can reduce your risk of developing health problems and improve your overall quality of life.

THAT CAN WAIT

UNTIL TOMORROW

LAZINESS

Myth: People can't be ill one minute and not the next, they are just lazy!

Truth: Some conditions have varying degrees of debilitation of the person.

It is essential for small business owners to recognize that employees with chronic ill-health are not lazy. Prioritising the health of employees can ultimately benefit the success and sustainability of a small business.

Understanding the distinction between ill-health and laziness is crucial for creating a supportive and inclusive work environment. According to the Oxford dictionary, the definition of laziness is the quality of being unwilling to work or use energy, in work terms, the person may have the ability to achieve great work yet that person lacks the willingness and motivation to do so. There are several signs to lookout for to spot a lazy employee, these include:

Task avoidance – The employee may appear busy by moving around the office or taking time to respond to questions and deadlines, while their calendar and results fail to reflect otherwise. The employee tends to also mention how busy they are all the time too.

Procrastination – Very similar to task avoidance is procrastination, but instead of looking busy, the employee takes their time during breaks, often returning late or offering to take on more tasks 'outside' of the one they are often being paid to perform. For example, choosing to take letters to the post office, and taking longer than other employees have in the past.

Delegation overload – Lazy employees will often ask others to assist them with the work, moving the bulk in their direction. If the work presented is vastly differently to their usual level of work, it is possible that others have been involved. Sometimes lazy employees will ask junior/apprentice/support staff to create the work but take all the accolades for themselves. It is important to investigate this if you are concerned as you may have staff being unutilised, manipulated and disillusioned by the company or more so the lazy employee who could be developed into an amazing employee if managed correctly.

Body language and tone – How a person holds themselves around others is telling, motivated staff will sound excited and act energetically in tasks, while laziness is often viewed with slouching, sounding bored, taking their mobile phone to the bathroom, or continuing to pick it up throughout the day.

Stressed out – Stress doesn't always come from a heavy workload, as guilt can be overwhelming. Avoiding work can take as much effort and sometimes more effort than the actual work would take should they have started. Listen and watch the employee to see how the stress reflects on their workload.

It is important to be aware that lazy employees can be developed into highly motivated employees through positive management. The employee may be struggling with the task or have issues at home. By having a positive discussion with the employee to pinpoint the issue causing the lack of motivation, there is no reason to consider removing them.

But how does this differ from the people who may describe themselves as ill on some workdays to perform tasks, yet they have been 'seen' outside of the office doing more?

Certain conditions for example Fibromyalgia as mentioned in Chapter 2, can impact the person in different ways throughout their life, with over thirty symptoms associated with the condition from widespread pain to conjunctivitis (*pink/dry eyes*). There are days where the person can 'manage' their symptoms to perform tasks to the point that to those unaware of their personal circumstances would question their illness/disability, while other days the same person may struggle to dress themselves on other occasions. The level of personal management required to maintain a 'regular' living can take a toll on the person both mentally and physically and spikes or flares (*as they are often called*) can be triggered at any point throughout the day or night.

How does a Flare mimic laziness?

As mentioned, the key signs to lookout for are – Looking stressed, sounding bored, sloughing, avoiding tasks, extended breaks, low quality, and late work. To the untrained eye, the employee suffering through a flare will appear drained, distant, unmotivated, struggling with their work and taking extended breaks, and therefore hitting the lazy employee flags, however these differences are telling.

With lazy employees the work and the signs do not differ throughout the task, it is 100% the same approach every day. While the ill employee's journey often will. You may have a highly motivated employee that for 70% of their time, their work is exceptional/very good, they seem happy, they don't take extended breaks and may work through them, however for the other 30% they seem like a completely different person even on the exact same tasks.

It is therefore vital that the supervisor/manager is aware of any underlying conditions and how they impact on the person's ability to perform their role. If the employee is a valued and experienced member of the team, their 70% may be of a higher quality to the company than another's 100% and working with that employee to maintain their levels could save the company in the long run compared to replacing their experience with someone in the hope of securing 100% throughout.

Burning Profits

ONE SIZE FITS

ALL, RIGHT?

Diversity

Myth: It costs too much money to adjust the workplace for every specific need.

Truth: A quality EDI workplace policy is less expensive long term and benefits everyone.

By fostering a culture of empathy and flexibility, businesses can promote employee well-being and productivity. Empathy and understanding, combined with practical solutions, can lead to a more engaged and motivated workforce.

Companies are required by law to make reasonable adjustments to not breach Equality and Diversity standards.

EQUALITY – Treating people fairly with value and respect irrespective of their natural characteristics.

DIVERSITY – Creating a culture which values the individual's differences for the benefit of others, society, and organisations.

Although the legal aspect tends to lend itself more to those with a recognised disability, this is increasingly becoming open to those with long term health conditions. In terms of disability, should an employee require a wheelchair, it would be the company's responsibility to make their premises wheelchair friendly where reasonable, for example, clearing obstacles around the office, installing ramp/lifts where possible, and priority parking close to the entrance.

A benefit for some businesses for adding these features (*such as shops and restaurants*) opens the opportunity to cater for the disabled market, often known as the Purple Pound and worth more than £274 billion per year *(See Bib 1.1)*

What is reasonable will depend on several factors, including the size and nature of the organization, among other factors.

These adjustments don't always require physical changes to the organisation. These can include:

Additional Training – Some learners may take longer to retain all the information provided or to have the training to suit their training needs, for example visual compared to reading information etc.

Hybrid working – A mix of in-office and remote working, depending on the needs of the role.

Changing the sickness policy – Traditionally most polices see growing levels of intervention depending on sick leave. For example, being sick on Monday, returning to work on Tuesday to be off again on Wednesday will be considered two periods of sickness, which can lead to warning and in certain cases dismissal. By adjusting this policy for those employees with ill-health will help both the company and employee long term. One consideration is to split the periods into clusters – if the employee has a flare that can impact on them over a 2-week period but is needed to attend on certain days throughout the period, those split periods could be considered a cluster and only count as one sick period. What will often happen is that the employee will rest/recover in-between the important days to ensure the vital work is not missed while still managing their condition.

Formatting documents – Adapting the manuals into audio, braille, or alternative formats, will include all employees, regardless of their needs.

There are many more examples to how companies can adhere to EDI Polices without breaking the bank, through discussions before employees need them and with them should the requirement occur. In providing reasonable adjustments, communication is key. *(See Bib 1.2)*

Burning Profits

Burning Profits

WHY DO YOU

BOTHER?

BURDEN

Myth: Chronically-ill people are a burden on the economy.

Truth: Chronically-ill people can provide so much to both companies and the wider community.

Many chronically ill individuals often struggle with feelings of being a burden to others, including their employers and colleagues. This perception can significantly impact their self-esteem and confidence in the workplace.

Employers should recognise the value that these individuals bring to the team, as their unique perspectives and resilience can greatly benefit the company and the broader community. By creating a supportive and inclusive work environment, business owners can empower chronically ill employees to thrive and contribute meaningfully, thereby fostering a culture of empathy and understanding within the organisation.

The impact of feeling like a Burden:

Self-esteem - In a study by Wirth, Allen & Zitek entitled Feeling Like a Burden, Self-compassion buffers against the Negative effects of a Poor Performance, the link between feeling burdensome and social interaction within teams could create and exasperate poor-performance, resulting in an endless cycle of negativity and reduced productivity. *(See Bib 2.1)*

Being ill, the employee faces life changes, tasks that were once easy are now time consuming and, in some cases, painful to perform. This loss of self, or loss of one's past self, has more of an impact on the employee's mental health than the physical which is often associated with chronic pain. Questioning their ability to perform to the standard they previously were accustomed too, in addition to the misunderstanding colleagues may have to the impact of ill-health on the employee long-term due to the misconceptions mentioned previously, will often make the employee question themselves further and massively damage their self-esteem and unless addressed can put the employee into despair, impacted their life outside of the workplace. With low self-esteem, productivity can be vastly reduced causing further frustrations throughout the team and organization.

Confidence – As mentioned above, the workplace confidence of the employee can be massively reduced over time if the employee isn't supported by both the organization and their colleagues. Having confident employees can often produce happy employees, and when employees are happy at work, productivity can rise, improving the organisation's profitability.

The negatives of the burden of ill-health of the employee are obvious, but the value of chronically ill individuals in the workplace cannot be overlooked.

Resilience – Being chronically ill comes with its' challenges but with the challenge comes strength. Being in pain 24/7 allows the employee to understand their body through self-management, with that understanding they push their bodies hard to fight through the day that often minor conditions such as colds for example tend not to impact them as much as it may non-chronic employees. This is often due to them battling against being a burden and fear of being rejected by organisations and their peers but can be to prove to themselves that they are still valuable to their workplace and colleagues.

Innovation – Illness is not subjective, it does not discriminate, it can strike at any point, and everyone is at risk. It is a scary fact, however with fear comes opportunity. As a business/organisation it is important to innovate regularly to survive, yet that innovation tends to be external rather than internal, however by engaging with chronically ill employees and tapping into their unique perspectives to work and the traversing the workplace, employers can make the adaptations that could save them thousands in the long term by pre-empting the impact of future illness that could affect anyone including the employer themselves. These adaptions could be as simple as hybrid-working, all the way up to building structures.

Learning opportunities – As mentioned above, the feeling of being a burden does not just impact the employee in terms to their individual work, but how they interact with their colleagues, and with the various misconceptions of ill-health often apparent in the workplace, it is vital that organisations provide support to the employee, but that they also provide their colleagues with similar opportunities and help them understand the difference between support and favouritism. People do not want to think that one employee is getting more than they are, especially if they feel that the employee in question appears to be performing at a lower level than they are. By providing training and information on ill-health and how it can impact their colleagues in and out of the workplace, it will help them recognise the struggle and positives associated with being chronically ill-health and how their own approach could impact on them in both the long and short term. This training should not be limited to chronic ill-health and should include finances, mental health, and in some circumstances parenting. An understanding workplace is a positive one, with employees and employers working together for the betterment of the organisation and their collective futures.

JUST PART OF THE

ENDLESS MACHINE

CULTURE

Myth: There are not that many people with ill-health in most workplaces.

Truth: 1 in every 7 (6.8) people in the workplace have either physical or mental ill-health at some point in their employment.

We've talked about workplace culture but what is it really?

Workplace or organisation culture relates to the attitudes and behaviours of the people within the workplace. These can be defined and impacted from the environment including policies, goals, values, company mission and leadership of the organisation.

It is important that everyone or mostly everyone within the organisation align with the organisation to improve productivity, profitability, and overall employee retention. Worst case scenario for organisations is to move into an **'US vs THEM'** situation, for example removing employee benefits as a cost-cutting exercise while at the same time increasing productivity demands.

The **US vs THEM** scenario doesn't always mean it is employers vs employees, instead employees could create their own mini collectives and battle other members of the organisation. Like we mentioned in the **BURDEN** chapter, if an employee(s) believe they are being treated differently to others, this mentality can begin to emerge, this is why it is vital to create a positive approach to internal bridging, learning and inclusivity, remember, most misconceptions and misunderstandings come from a lack of accurate information and evidence, in addition to the approach to how it is provided.

According to the charity Mental Health Foundation approximately 1 in every 6.8 employees (*14.7%*) will experience mental health problems in the workplace, with an additional 4.9% attributed to long-term health problems. In comparison, a global study conducted by Gallup in 2019 uncovered that out of the world's one billion full-time employees approximately 85% of workers were dissatisfied with their job, that is seventeen dissatisfied employees in every twenty, driving home the need for alignment and understanding. (*See Bib 3.1*)

It is simple mathematics, a happy employee is a productive one, and the more productive employees an organisation has then more can be achieved and high profits garnered, ensuring everyone benefits in both the long and short-term. As mentioned above in the Gallup poll, only 15% of employees were satisfied with their employment, with most of this coming back to the culture of the organisation. When employees feel appreciated and supported, they want to do more for the organisation and commit to the mission, however, that doesn't mean an organisation needs to lose the competitive nature of the workplace, but rather than making it feel combative, it can be developed into something more collaborative. An example of a combative workplace culture are high sales companies, for example automobile sales, where being the no1 seller is the number one goal for the employees, when the company just wants as many vehicles sold as possible.

If salesperson A constantly makes fifteen sales and salesperson B 8 sales in this combative environment, salesperson A will continually be rewarded at the expense of salesperson B, who in turn may become disillusioned with the company and leave. Now some organisations may say that this happens and a sales person can always be replaced but there is no guarantee that salesperson C will sell the same or more vehicles, they may only sell 5, not including the month it may take to replace salesperson B and train up salesperson C, which doesn't directly impact on sales person A, they are still pulling in their 10, but now they only need to bring in 6 or 7, in the end, the loser is the company, who have now lost out on approximately 32 sales over the month, and an additional 3 a week thereafter. By making the culture more collaborative salesperson A and B both bring in twenty-three sales and the team are rewarded with additional praise or bonus to salesperson A. That additional bonus or praise is warranted and accepted by the team because everyone was rewarded for the collective sales rather than punished for not being no1.

Having happy employees is one aspect of a positive workplace culture but there are larger and more devastating consequences of getting this wrong.

Discrimination – The Equality Act protects nine characteristics including age, race, sex, sexual orientation, gender reassignment, marriage and civil partnership, pregnancy and maternity, religion or belief, and disability. In context, some chronic illness conditions are either/both sex and disability specific, making it vital employers understand the ramifications of not understanding this information. Employers that create poor workplace cultures are at a higher risk of being liable for any discriminatory actions by the employees that occur during their employment with the organisation, and it is the employer's responsibility to ensure that all their employees (including themselves) are aware of what is and is not acceptable to other employees protected by this Act. (*See Bib 3.2*)

Mental Health and Stress – With 14.9% of the organisation's employees at risk of mental health problems, an unhealthy working environment will more than likely increase the speed and number of cases within the organisation,

Bullying and harassment – Some employees may only see this as workplace 'banter', but it is important to recognise that it can have deeper repercussions if it is not addressed early, before it moves from mutual 'banter' into the realms of civil and then criminal policy breaches.

Damages to the organisation for failing to adhere to this Act and improve their workplace culture can include employment tribunals with expensive legal fees, fines and compensation, bad publicity and a loss in sales/clients/suppliers, and staff losses.

The bottom line is that improving the workplace's culture doesn't need to be expensive, but it does require work and communication.

Burning Profits

NICE OF YOU

TO SHOW UP

ABSENTEEISM

Myth: People who are chronically ill are always off sick.

Truth: On average more sick days are lost to minor sickness absence than long-term sickness.

It is a bold statement to say that people who are long-term sick have fewer sick days and have less impact than those with minor sickness, but there is so much more to unpack than just the period, to break this down we need to understand the difference between the two.

Short-term illness – Short-term illness/conditions can be split into two areas, **MINOR** & **MAJOR**.

MINOR – Minor illnesses/conditions are the typical conditions associated with being ill, these include colds, headaches, and stomach upsets. They are often accompanied with physical symptoms that the onlooker would understand that the person was sick, such as a running nose, and coughing.

Minor conditions can result in sick days from 24 hours to up to 4 weeks depending on the severity of the illness. The period is also influenced by the contagion aspect of the condition, headaches are not often contagious while colds often are.

MAJOR – Major conditions relate more to surgeries, accidents, and acute medical conditions. Again, the symptoms are visible to onlookers such as bandaged limbs, and physical changes.

Major conditions can result in sick days up to 28 days with pay. Depending on the severity of the condition, a major condition can develop into a chronic or long-term condition over time.

Long-term illness – Long-term illnesses/conditions are often called chronic or invisible illnesses, chronic refers to the consistency of the symptoms recurring, and they are often invisible to the onlooker, and in some cases invisible to some medical testing. *(see chapter 2)*

The frequency of the symptoms and sick periods can last from a few hours to several weeks, but they are still mostly viewed as short-term illnesses in terms of sick leave or in some cases dismissed.

According to statistics by the UK Government, the estimate number of absences in 2022 were a massive 185.6 million workdays lost, equating to approximately 5.7 days per worker, per year, or 133 days per business, per year. *(See Bib 4.1)*

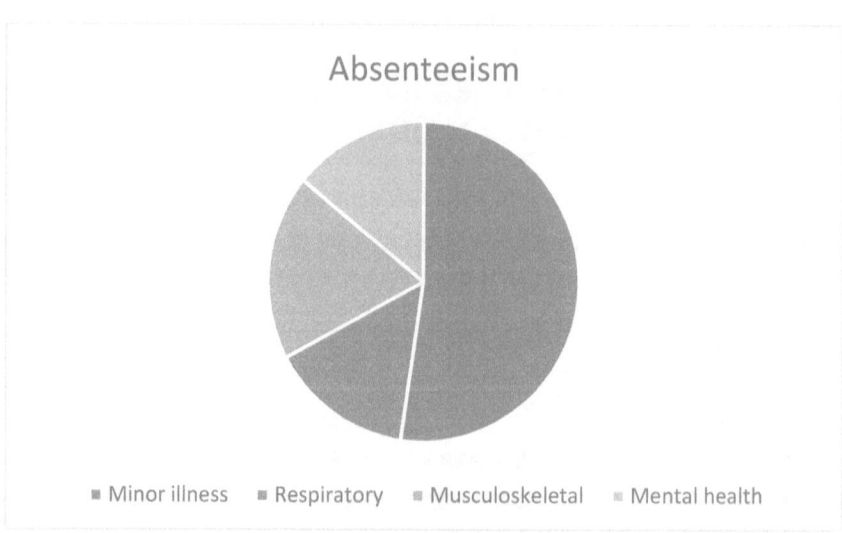

Minor illnesses such as colds took top spot of a huge 29.3%, compared to respiratory on 8.3%, musculoskeletal at 10.5%, and Mental Health at 7.9%, other conditions were listed at 23.8% which included both major and long-term conditions.

This saw an increase in sick days compared to 2021 of approximately 30%, it is important to note that the COVID years were most prominent in the UK between March 2020 and December 2021, making the rise more concerning for companies and organisations world-wide.

The Novuna Business Cash Flow reported that the estimated financial cost to the UK economy during this period was more than £20 billion pounds. (*See Bib 4.2*)

One of the main differences between short and long-term conditions other than the above statistics, is the impact on the rest of the employees and company. Going back to the automobile sales company in chapter 6, we can see the impact more clearly through two scenarios.

Scenario 1 - At the company there are eleven employees, the manager, finance lead, vehicle detailer, maintenance lead, HR Consultant, two technicians, a customer service representative, and three salespeople. Currently salesperson A is the top salesperson with fifteen sales a week, compared with salesperson B with eight sales, and salesperson C with five sales.

Salesperson A develops a chronic condition that impacts on their ability to stand for extended periods, making it increasingly difficult to make sales, knocking their confidence and needing to take longer breaks and some days off. With the pressure to compete with the other salespeople increasing, salesperson A takes extended leave for 2 weeks on health grounds.

None of the other employees are impacted by salesperson A's condition but find themselves down fifteen sales per week while salesperson A recovers.

LOSS – 15 sales a week, total thirty sales.

Scenario 2 – In this scenario, salesperson A does not have a chronic condition but catches a flu-like virus. At first salesperson A can continue at work but after a few days needs to take some sick leave to recover. During those few days, salesperson B, the customer service representative, and both technicians develop the virus and need to take time off, before the end of the week, seven of the ten employees have the virus resulting in sales not being processed, appointments being missed. In total, the impact costs the company 2 weeks of sales.

LOSS – 28 sales per week, total fifty-six sales.

Both scenarios show a loss in sales, but the short-term condition is larger due to the compounding nature of the condition impacting others. But in both scenarios the overall loss could be reduced, if the company have policies in place for reducing the spread of illness and have opportunities in place for salesperson A to perform their job differently or taking their skills and experience to mentor and train both salespeople B & C into improving their numbers to make up their shortfall.

In terms of absenteeism, it is important that everyone is aware of both the individual organisations polices and legalities regarding sick leave in the UK *(other countries may differ)*.

- According to the Gov.uk website, and unless noted differently in the organisations polices, employees can take up to seven off sick without needing to provide a doctor's note, this includes non-working days. *(See Bib 4.5)*

- After 7 days, the employee is required to provide their employer a doctor's note, often called a 'fit' or 'sick' note. The fit note will inform the employer that the employee is either fit/able to return to work, or not, often with further information on how the employer can support the employee in returning. Employers should retain a copy of the note, leaving the original with the employee. These notes **MUST** be provided by a healthcare professional and may often incur a charge, chargeable to the employee.

- Should the employer accept, then other forms of proof of

sickness can be provided by an Allied Health Professional via an AHP form.

- Organisations with more than five employees **MUST** have a Health & Safety policy in place and all employees are aware of, this document must provide information regarding their policy towards sick leave.

- Some organisations may also include a 'Return to Work' interview for employees who have taken sick leave, to discuss the nature of their illness, and any steps that need to be taken to reduce the situation being repeated in the future.

- While on sick leave and depending on the organisation's policy, the employee may retain full, or part pay. If this is not provided, then employees are paid Statutory Sick Pay (**SSP**) of approximately £110 a week for up to 28 weeks, from the fourth pay off sick, paid for by the employer.

- Should the employee be off sick for longer than the stated 28 weeks, the SSP will cease, and the employee would need to apply for other state benefits.

- There is no maximum period of sickness absence, but the employer should give all employees a reasonable period to return to work.

- Employees can be dismissed for continual and frequent sick leave; however, it is important that all steps are taken to assist the employee back to work first, failure to do this can result in expensive workplace tribunals and disputes.

It is important to consider all the eventualities of retaining or dismissing an employee before making any decisions over their employment, as experience and ability can be harder and more costly to replace than a legal case in the long run.

WHAT'S ON

YOUR MIND?

MINDSET

Myth: People with long- term health conditions are just weak-minded.

Truth: Fighting a long-term health condition takes an enormous amount of strength both mentally and physically.

There are several misconceptions between ill-health and mental strength, these include –

Stress of work – Unless the condition of the employee is known or discussed, the employer may be unaware of the employee's condition for some time. That employee may exhibit good attendance, be highly motivated at work and produce great work, while outside of the organisation their personal stress and struggle is highly noticeable to friends and family. Some employees' only break from their struggles may be at their employment, where they can focus on the tasks of their job. Employers may notice this in some employees that unlike others tend to remain in work for as long as possible.

Weak-minded – The term 'Man-up' was until recent years used on men who took sick leave or expressed emotions such as sadness, the fallacy that men must remain 'strong' and quiet throughout their lives, subduing their emotions has statically led to an increase in male suicides with 4 in every 5 suicides being men under 35 years old. Men have been societal driven to believe they are the providers of the family and asking for help will make them less of a man in the eyes of their family and peers. Health conditions can be caused by a multitude of factors from life experiences including abuse, biological factors such as their genetics, their family history, and triggers for example a reaction to surgery. By breaking this history of weaknesses and asking for help can take more strength than it would to continue in silence.

These misconceptions can lead into stigma and stereotypes when it comes to ill-health and employment.

Stigma occurs when the person is defined by what they do/where they are from rather than who they are as an individual in a negative way. They are poor, they have cancer, or they are psychotic rather than have psychosis etc.

There are four main types of stigmas that include, self-stigma, professional-stigma, public-stigma, and institutional-stigma, but there can be others, including structural or workplace-stigma. Workplace-stigma occurs when an organisations policies and practices result in the unfair treatment of people who have lived or are living with a health condition.

Much like stigmas, stereotypes work on the negative thoughts and beliefs of people about others and labelling them a certain way, however, unlike stigmas that are always negative, stereotypes are often wrong or partially wrong. The stigma is enforced by the stereotype, for example, all people with a mental illness are psychopathic, and people with chronic illnesses are just lazy. It is vital that employers have training in place to ensure stigmas and stereotypes are removed or do not start within the organisation, to ensure future issues as mentioned in other chapters arise.

In a study by Schielder and Weisz in 2018, it was discovered that those people who developed a 'Growth Mindset' had improved abilities to cope with stress and anxiety compared to those who did not. A person's mindset is the key to hold the person perceives themselves within the world, their values, their dreams/goals, intelligence, and abilities. Those with a 'fixed' mindset in terms of chronic health may always see the negative side of their situation and view events of 'proof' of their beliefs. (*See Bib 5.1*)

Proof – *"I was unable to attend the show because I was in pain."*

Fixed mindset – *"I'm always missing things because of my pain."*

Future thinking – *"I'll never be able to attend shows in the future so why bother, I'm useless."*

Many employees that continue in work or seek out work opportunities would look at these situations with their Growth Mindset, switching the narrative –

Proof? – *"I was unable to attend the show because I was in pain."*

Growth Mindset – *"If I look into the triggers that caused my pain on that night, I might be able to make the next one."*

Future thinking – *"There will be times I miss things I want to do, but in time and by managing my condition, I'll be able to do so much more in the future."*

The difference is staggering, the fixed mindset will focus on the negative, it happened before so it will happen again, I cannot change things. While the Growth Mindset, breaks down the negatives to find solutions to ensure a change occurs. In terms of people with chronic health conditions, a Growth Mindset is key to maintaining a positive life balance, they understand this will not 'cure' them, but instead allow them to do more in their new lives as a person with a long-term health condition. A Growth Mindset is not just associated with ill-health and can be adaptable for other forms of life and business, with some of the most successful people in the world adopting this method of growth and life.

Taking myself as a chronic, my symptoms include:

Extreme fatigue: Struggling to stay awake at times.

Widespread pain: In all joints but mainly hands and legs.

Conjunctivitis – Regular dry eyes making it difficult to read or see for 1–2-day periods.

Hypermobility – Knee and elbow joints can unlock from the sockets.

Brain fog – Forgotten simple words and can impact on speech.

Irritable bowel syndrome (IBS) – Stomach and bowel complications.

There are others but these are the primary issues that I will endure either daily or frequently.

During the first few months of having the condition I was unemployed, taking time away from my University studies, going through a divorce and recent infertility news, it was a lot and there were times my fixed mindset took every negative and supercharged it, I was told I'd never hold down a regular job again and my life would be a regular struggle, it was still a further 18 months before any diagnoses. However, following a fixed proof event I discovered the mindset and made the appropriate mind to physical changes. Those changes led to work in business development, the NHS, local council, and eventually The Chronic Edge. I still have all the above symptoms and more, but I understand the demands of my body and continuingly amend maintain a positive life.

Extreme tiredness – I will reduce late nights to create a regular pattern of sleep and take a power nap when needed.

Widespread pain – Pain comes in levels from easily ignored to impossible, I have gloves and gels for my hands, and medication or rest for the higher levels.

Conjunctivitus – In most evenings I will wear a heated eye mask and use sprays and drops, reducing screen time.

Hypermobility – I am more careful with my movements and have changed my exercise habits to strength based to create stronger joints and fibres, they still occur but have become less frequent.

Brain fog – I take certain supplements and look at what I eat and drink, I also listen to music or sit in silence to slow my mind down until the fog settles.

IBS – Food and drink intake is considered, reducing triggering items.

It doesn't stop them from ever occurring but when I look at how I was during the first 6-8 months, the change is massive, and none of that would have happened without support and a change in my mindset.

By providing access to wellbeing support to your employees, the journey to a stronger mindset is within reach to everyone before they may need it, reducing issues should they occur later in life.

Burning Profits

Burning Profits

THAT'S A BIT RICH,

COMING FROM YOU

HIGH COSTS

Myth: Wellness programmes and long-term health support is too expensive.

Truth: Well-being in the workplace doesn't have to come with a price tag but is far cheaper than not having one.

There are several misconceptions about what wellness in the workplace means to an organisation, these include –

Wellness is only physical – The association of wellbeing and physical health is advertised all over the world, with gym memberships and bring your bike to work schemes, this brings us back to several previous chapters to why, the benefits of physical wellbeing can be SEEN, exercise creates physical changes, and if you look good then in turn you must feel good too. However, again as we've mentioned, while the physical will help in some areas, without the mental side, they may fail before even getting started. A rounded approach to wellness that includes both mental and physical is the best option for stainability.

Wellness support is a one size fits all – The only fixed similarity between everyone in the organisation is that they are all employees of the organisation. They will have different personalities, goals, dreams, lifestyles, and hobbies outside of the organisation, therefore taking a one-size-fits-all approach to a wellness package means there will be employees that just don't fit in with what is on offer. Organisations need to consider their company's culture and ask their employees for their opinions, the best route to employee wellness is to do it with them and not for them.

Programs are easy to implement – This will often put off employers from implementing a programme, they just want to pick a package, make the payment and watch as their employees start to improve, but just like the point above, life doesn't work that way, and it can be more expensive making mistakes trying to find the right package than it would be without a comprehensive strategy. The best approach to adding a wellness scheme is to look at it like a new product or service for your clients/customers. If organisations speak with their employees, research the various options, work with an expert, consider their workplace culture and the goals of the programme, then the success of the implementation will be greater.

Wellness is expensive – As above, it can be depending on what the organisation is looking to achieve long-term, but as discussed the dissatisfaction rate of employees is in excess of 80% world-wide, creating a lull in productivity and reduction in profits, therefore adding a package and other benefits that turn those dissatisfied employees into happy and positive employees can create a positive rate of return long-term, resulting in greater productivity and profitability. Remember, not everyone wants a pool table in their office.

Wellness programs can replace other benefits – The social focus of wellness in the workplace has somewhat clouded some organisations in shifting from traditional employee benefits to implement wellness ones, however this is not the right approach for a successful workplace culture. Traditional benefits like healthcare, days out, paid holidays, and bonus etc are still vital for an organisation's employees, a wellness program should be viewed as an add-on to the additional benefits rathe than a replacement. There is no point in offering a gym membership if the employee's childcare vouchers are removed, as the impact both mentally and financially for the employee could be catastrophic.

Wellness programs are a quick fix – That would be amazing if it were though, a few days after implementing the package and all the employees are now happy and have added an additional 25% to their productivity, but ever change can take time. If employees are part of the process from the start of the process, then the organisation is creating a co-produced approach to wellness that once implemented the employees will engage with sooner, however the opposite can occur if they are ignored in favour of an organisational preference. Wellness programmes are about sustainable long-term growth of the employees within the organisation and that can take time to bear fruit.

British hospitality company *Disroom* were voted Glassdoor's number 12 in 2022's Best Place to Work in the UK list. Their benefits package includes:

Competitive industry salaries.
Total distribution of service charges.
Fully trained managers in Mental Health first aid.
24-hour confidential counselling helpline.
Discounted memberships, classes, and other fitness sessions from local gyms and studios.

They also reward long-term employees (*5-years*) with a 5-day immersive food tour of Bombay. (*See Bib 5.1*)

Breaking down *Disroom's* package, organisations are looking at –

Fair wage offer.
Profit sharing or bonus.
A training package to improve skills and support.
Working with a charity or company that provides a specialist service.

Strengthening bonds with the local community and companies, to improve fitness and wellbeing.

When broken down, their package doesn't seem as expensive as some by believe it needs to be, it is about looking at what the organisation's employees want and researching ways to achieve it, also stronger bonds can improve customer numbers and public representation.

Consider the cost of an effective wellness programme against the cost of absenteeism as a factor in the decision to implement a programme.

If we took our automobile dealership into consideration, the cost per employee per year can be anything from £100 - £1500, taking an average of around £800 a year for each employee, the total cost per year for this company is £8000 a year for all ten employees.

But when we put it against the potential loss of the two previous scenarios and took the dissatisfaction of employees into consideration too in terms of salesperson A vs salesperson B, things get interesting.

For this example, we will be pricing the cost of each vehicle at an average of £5000 each. Salesperson A - £75K for fifteen sales, salesperson B - £40K for eight sales, and salesperson C - £25K for five sales.

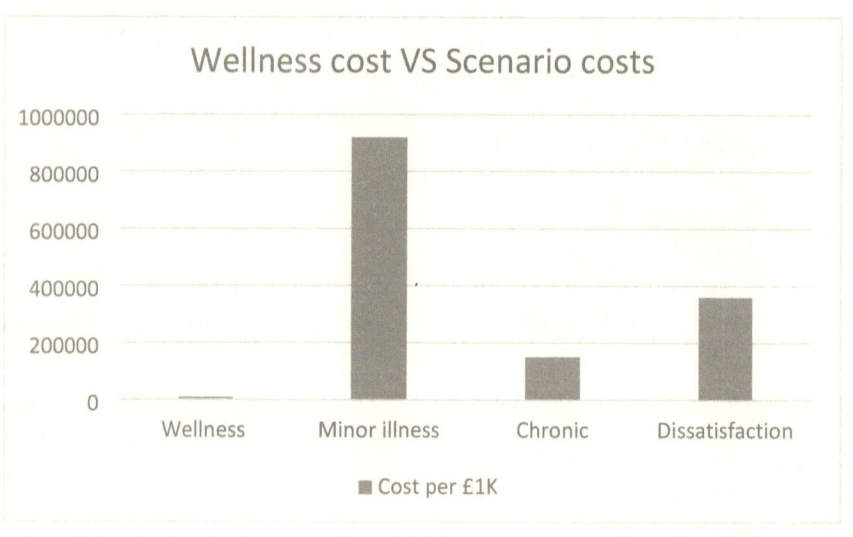

Looking at the loss over the year in each scenario, it is evident that the £8000 a year investment in the wellbeing of the organisation's workforce is minor compared to the potential outcomes of the other issues from illness to cultural dissatisfaction within the team.

Do a cost analysis for yourself when looking at the cost vs investment, what might seem like wasted expenditure outside of salaries, might be what is needed to supercharge the business for years to come.

The bottom line is –

PROTECTING THE TEAM, PROTECTS THE BUSINESS!

Burning Profits

I THINK IT'S TIME

WE TALKED.

COMMUNICATION

Myth: It is easy for an employee to discuss their needs with an employer.

Truth: There is a lot of fear and stigma around discussing health with an employer before and during their employment.

We've talked a lot about the stigma and perception around health conditions and the workplace throughout this book, with the main method of supporting employees long-term always coming down to one simple word – **COMMUNICATION**.

As employers may never know what is happening in an employee's life without being told, but the employee needs to understand and be fully assured that when and more importantly IF they do, that they will be treated with respect, kindness, and support. The fear is often that the employer will stand on the side of the misconception and stigma, focusing on the negatives to what the employee cannot do, rather than the positives and opportunities that could arise from them being open over their needs.

This occurs more during the interview process, and more so in people with disabilities. Applications nowadays have a tick box for applicants to tick to confirm that they have a disability/illness that will impact on their daily lives, and often by ticking the box, they are guaranteed an interview, regardless of their suitability for the role. There are multiple problems with this method.

"If I tick the box, they will interview me, but I won't

get the job." – By ticking the box, the fear is that it is a method of keeping on the right side of the Equality Act, but they will be turned down for the role because of it.

"How do I know if they want me, or they have to interview me?" – It is a guaranteed interview regardless of suitability. The person doesn't know whether they are one step closer to the employment, or that they are simply a tick-box exercise.

"I don't want to be judged before I have the chance to talk to them." – Some people will choose not to tick the box, because they want to be judged on their own merit, or that they'd rather discuss their condition in person to remove any potential misconceptions. The issue with this, is that they haven't mentioned it when requested and may feel they come across as untrustworthy.

"I'm not sure if I should tick it, because my symptoms won't impact my job all of the time like the box states."
– The boxes tend to ask applicants to list any conditions that impact them daily, as we have seen throughout this book, symptoms have levels and what may be extreme one day, is manageable other, and therefore does not fit the brief.

While the box cannot be changed currently, it is something for employers to consider, and look to address any concerns potentially employees may have. For example, if this is an applicant that the company is interested in hiring from the interview, before it ends, mention the amazing wellbeing package the organisation has in-place for employees and the support on offer, emphasising on the importance of knowing about any needs in advance to make the appropriate steps to support that employee should they be successful. This support in advance can help a potential employee open-up to any concerns and ask questions.

We've mentioned that addressing an employee's health concerns is crucial, and it is essential that employers and managers manage such discussions with both care and professionalism. But how?

- By creating an environment within the workplace, which will encourage open communication and promotes trust. This will help the employee to feel more comfortable discussing their health issues and seek assistance in what support they need.

- Prioritise confidentiality and ensure that personal data shared during those discussions remain confidential between those stated and agreed to before the meeting begins. An employee may request someone accompanies them to the meeting, this can help them relax and should be allowed if possible.

- Education is key in improving communication, ensure that training is up to date with the relevant health and safety regulations, to assist you in providing accurate guidance and support.

- Have a wellness programme or support information available to employees, to help support their needs both mentally and physically. Ensure that the employee is aware of how to access this support and help them with any questions they may have over the process.

- Be empathic and understanding, while maintaining a professional and clear tone. Employees with health concerns are not looking for sympathy, instead they want to feel understood and empowered that their condition will not cost them their employment.

By implementing these practical tips, employers can navigate health-related conversations with employees successfully, fostering a healthy and productive work environment. In addition, by having clear guidance in place and training, employees will feel secure, which can lead to an increase in job satisfaction and productivity.

WHAT WOULD YOU DO

TO SAVE A LIFE?

RETENTION SAVES LIVES

Throughout this book you will have learnt about several myths, misconceptions, and stigmas about ill-health and how it relates to employment, the costs of wellness investment, and how that investment cost relates to the surprising costs of not having support in place early.

It isn't a one size fits all approach, or a competition over who has the best package in place, it is about understanding your employees to assist them in being the best version of themselves, because if they feel their best both mentally and physically, but also understood and wanted by their organisation, then their commitment to the organisation will rise and in turn their productivity, ensuring that everyone benefits.

This book talks about how retention can save lives, but what do we mean by that?

- **Saving the Employee** – Traversing this book you will have come to understand that living with a health condition is extremely difficult for the individual. Their life may have changed drastically, and the tasks they could once do with ease, are now harder or impossible.

  If you look back at the misconceptions and stigma surrounding health conditions, you can understand the fear of loss regarding employment your employees may have had or currently have. Losing their job can have massive consequences for them moving forward, they could struggle to gain new employment from the fear of misunderstanding or believing they are burdensome, this can lead into further losses in terms of their home and increase their anxiety and potential depression.

  In a study by Lewis & Sloggett in 1998 (*See Bib 6.1*) entitled

Suicide, deprivation, and unemployment record linkage study looking at the association between suicide and socioeconomic status, unemployment and chronic illness, found that the association between suicide and unemployment was more important than any other socioeconomic metric, and although some potential important confounders were not adjusted for, their findings supported the idea that a lack of job security, and unemployment increased the risk of suicide. (*Note: the study included unemployed disabled people in the long-term ill category*).

By reducing the fear of losing their employment and increasing the positive culture within your organisation, the retention of experienced employees in a positive workplace environment, will in-turn strengthen job satisfaction, knowing that their condition will not impact on the organisation retaining their services, ultimately helping them maintain their existing life or helping them grow into their new one as they learn to live and strive with their health condition.

- **Saving the Organisation** – To some employers, their business is like their child, it becomes its' own entity as such, and the loss of a business feels like a death in the family. When organisations lose experienced employees through illness or to other companies, it can be extremely difficult to replace them. It is not as simple as replacing the body, there are so many other aspects to consider. The financial and time costs of the hiring process, including reading resumes, interviewing applicants, and the new starter process can take months before the new person can start the role, with no guarantee that they will remain in the post long-term, but you must also consider the experience loss, the former employee may already have had built strong relationships with clients, have a vast understanding of both the role and the organisations mission and values, that the new employee may take time to grow themselves.

But if you also take into account what we discussed in the culture chapter, by having a negative culture full of dissatisfied employees can lead to a reduction in productivity and more workforce losses, these continual losses can impact on the organisation's bottom line and lead to issues with your ability to trade effectively, this in-turn will have a knock-on effect with clients and suppliers, that if not addressed appropriately can lead ultimately into the closure of the organisation.

Retention of clients, relationships, and experienced employees is key to the survival of a business/organisation and understanding what can be achieved through positive communication of the support of employees either with a health condition or having protections in place should the organisation need to in the future, can save the business from becoming another failed statistic.

This information isn't about forcing employers into keeping employees or into paying millions of pounds on external services, but instead is about alleviating any concerns and dispelling myths about ill-health and employment, it is about how your organisations culture could be impacting your ability of getting the best out of your employees, and the positives that can be gained by communicating and working with your employees as people rather than parts of the organisation that could be replaced without much fuss.

Just remember that **RETENTION SAVES LIVES**, and how you interpret that in the future can make an incredible difference to everyone within your organisation for years to come.

Burning Profits

ARE YOU PREPARED TO GO TO WAR

FOR YOUR EMPLOYEES & ORGANISATION?

About the chronic edge

The Chronic Edge is all about unleashing your edge over your work, life or business for the better, after some time I realised that the Chronic Edge wasn't just my business but it is the edge I unleashed for myself.

My mission is to help bridge the gap between the so called 'economically inactive' and employers, by helping the individual discovery their worth, and supporting companies in seeing their talents first.

COMPANIES: We help companies understand the importance of working with their chronically ill employees and how to reinforce the organisation with the skills needed should before an employee becomes sick.

How do we do this?

- **Book** – Good job, you've already done that bit, well done!

- **Courses** – I have some courses that go deeper into some of the areas mentioned in this book, to help you and your team learn more about the importance of retention, culture, and the impact of ill-health on productivity, profitability, and survival.

- **Custom Packages** – This can be in the form of workshops, talks, or 1-1/group project work.

INDIVIDUALS: In addition to helping companies, The Chronic Edge offers support to individuals with chronic health conditions, with their motivation, accountability, and support needs.

How do we do this?

- **Book** – This one will help them understand that being chronically ill doesn't mean their career needs to be over.

- **Courses** – I Have some micro courses, and a mindset course for people looking to step into work or start their own business.

- **Free resources** – We have several free resources including our YouTube channel – Living on the Edge, where we share information and our podcast.

- **Custom Packages** – There are options for 1-1 or group work.

In addition to the website and YouTube channel, we have a shop for motivational merchandise, and donate 25% of our profits to both organisations looking co-productively support local communities, and chronically ill/neuro-diverse individuals start their own businesses.

Visit us at www.thechronicedge.co.uk

At The Chronic Edge, we understand that when it comes to chronic health, the war with your body can be a lonely one, but your battle doesn't need to be fought alone. Stand strong Warrior.

HAS THIS GIVEN YOU

SOME IDEAS?

About the Author

Since getting sick in late 2016, Elliot has gone on to work for multiple tech companies and the NHS.

In 2022 he launched the podcast Living on the Edge, and created The Chronic Edge, to help others unleash their own edge, working together with businesses in a place of understanding, co-production, and the opportunity for growth.

He resides in Fleetwood, Lancashire, UK with his wife Gill, with a passion for charity work and writing fiction.

Burning Profits

CAN I HAVE A

REFERENCE PLEASE?

Bibliography

1.1 – My Business need to be accessible and can I get funding: https://valleyheritage.org.uk/does-my-business-need-to-be-accessible-and-can-I-get-finding/

1.2 - Workplace guidance EDI: https://www.healthyworkinglives.scot/workplace-guidance/fair-treatment/equality-and-diversity/Pages/ill-health-and-disability.aspx

2.1 – Feeling like a Burden: https://self-compassion.org/wp-content/uploads/2021/11/Wirth-et-al-2020-Feeling-like-a-burden-Self-compassion-buffers-aga.pdf

3.1 – Gallup poll: https://staffsquared.com/blog/why-85-of-people-hate-their-jobs/#:~:text=A%20global%20poll%20conducted%20by,are%20unhappy%20in%20their%20jobs.

3.2 – Legal implications in culture: https://www.peoplemanagement.co.uk/article/1745534/what-are-the-legal-implications-of-poor-workplace-culture

4.1 – Sickness Absence 2022: https://www.ons.gov.uk/employmentandlabourmarket/peopleinwork/labourproductivity/articles/sicknessabsenceinthelabourmarket/2022#:~:text=The%20number%20of%20-working%20days,its%2Dpandemic%202019%20level.

4.2 – Novuna Cash Flow: https://www.novuna.co.uk/news-and-insights/business-cash-flow/sickness-absence-rate-in-the-uk-highest-since-2010/

4.3 – Taking sick leave: https://www.gov.uk/taking-sick-leave

5.1 – Growth Mindset: https://pubmed.ncbi.nlm.nih.gov/28921523/

6.1 – Disroom: https://employmenthero.com/uk/blog/british-companies-leading-workplace-wellness/

7.1 – Suicide, deprivation, and unemployment: record linkage study: https://www.ncbi.nlm.nih.gov/pmc/articles/PMC28707/

Burning Profits

www.ingramcontent.com/pod-product-compliance
Lightning Source LLC
Chambersburg PA
CBHW030451220526
45464CB00006B/2483